ADVICE

Carrington Allen

This edition first published in 2021
Carrington Allen
www.carringtonallen.com

ISBN 9 781678 0422 02

Printed in the United States of America

ACKNOWLEDGEMENTS

Thank you to Source for continued messages of clarity and guidance. I feel honored to be trusted with these words to share with you.

Thank you to my supportive and loving family. My children (Sophie, Matthew, and Emily) and my mother (Betty) for listening to these messages as they were coming through each day.

Thank you to my daughter, Emily, for her knowledge, patience, and clarity in assisting with editing these messages.

PREFACE

This book contains messages to inspire and guide you along your journey. May these words bring knowledge to erase fear and instill hope and joy into all of the opportunities that cross your paths.

This project is a result of many conversations I have had with Source. In January 2020, I began to clearly receive and write down these messages. (I use the name "Source" in this book at His request. Please feel free to substitute the name you feel most comfortable using: God, Almighty Father, Universe, etc.) In the months that followed, I compiled notebooks filled with helpful guidance and information to help my children physically heal and grow in faith.

I published my first book in August 2020, titled, *Love*. It was literally given to me as this book was, word by word. The writing process evolved from writing daily personal messages given to me to where I would sit and the words and images would just flow freely, page after page. Often the words would come so quickly I could hardly capture them on paper and had to begin recording them. I want you to know that you can do this too.

Perhaps you are not interested in writing a book, but you would like to receive daily guidance and inspiration. This process developed from daily practice. In December 2019, Source asked me to accept a 30-day challenge to follow my intuition for the month of January 2020. I accepted and the result was an increased closeness to Source and better "hearing." His messages became clear and easy and flowed throughout my day. I encourage you to consider that same 30-day challenge, it will change your life and enhance the lives around you. Please reach out to me if I can help you.

May these words gathered in the following pages bring you and your family peace, hope, and love.

Carrington

INTRODUCTION

Dear One,

If you had the opportunity to talk with me, Source, for one hour, what questions would you ask? Would you even seek my advice?

The following pages are filled with information that you most likely would not think to ask. This is advice you need to read, to soak in, and to reflect upon.

Your lives were meant to be filled with joy, love, and adventures that you anticipated before your arrival. I have passed these thoughts through to you via this book. I hope you will take the time after reading it to sit in silence and connect back with me. You and I created such a plan for your life, a good life, a good plan. Let me share with you the guidance you need to live your best life.

Much love and admiration,

Source

stepping stones

Life begins in such a way where you rely on your earthly hosts (parents and caretakers) to decide the direction of your first steps. And as you steady yourself and progress from walking to running, you often fall down.

At an early age you quickly learn that falling down is not the end of your adventure, it is nothing more than a slight setback. It is an opportunity to once again gain your balance and start over.

Throughout your young life, you stumble more than you fall because you have many around you reaching out to offer assistance. These may be parents, aunts, uncles, grandparents, or other family members. It might include coaches, teachers, neighbors, or even strangers. For when you are a child, people are often more likely to offer assistance.

And then you become a teen and insist on your independence. You balk at the idea of anyone offering you help, except perhaps your peers who you feel are the only ones that can relate to your current challenges.

This is a point where many begin to fall and expect more from their peers than their peers are capable of giving. The support you need is from an older soul, someone that actually understands the basics of life, the big picture, the overall scenario that you have most likely not yet seen.

So you fall and often let a stranger assist you when you have hit rock bottom, or in a moment of desperation, because you are too embarrassed at this point to turn to those closest to you to ask for guidance.

Who will understand you?

Who can you trust?

For this is also the point in your journey when you discover that you may have been deceived. Maybe this deception was created by a romantic connection, maybe a friend - anyone, really.

So, the moment that you step away to do it your way is also the moment you are disappointed by what another soul has done "to you."

The deception becomes real on more levels than you are aware.

Firstly, did anyone do anything to you? Or did something happen and you were part of it? You know forgiving the person is necessary to move on with your own journey, but it seems too difficult.

Life is a journey filled with duality. Every day you are given the opportunity to choose love or fear. It truly is that simple, but I digress. Let me just suggest that choosing forgiveness quickly and completely will move you along in a much better direction. But do you know where you are going? Do you have any idea where you came from?

What if life was like a visit to a new city? And you only had one day to enjoy as much as possible. Would you try to soak in each and every moment? Not caring if it was perfect, but instead just being a part of the experience? Like visiting places, you might plan your day to include seeing as much as possible. You might make a list of the things you are most interested in seeing and doing and make those a priority.

And if you traveled with a group, you may have to split up and go your own way to make sure that you were able to do what made you happiest, remembering this was your one chance to experience these things.

So, as you find yourself today, sitting there reading these words, think on this adventure. What do I want to do while I am here?

And then do it, make it a priority.

Because one day when you return you might just regret getting caught up in all of the reasons why you thought you couldn't do those things.

Who says you can't?

I say you can.

When you realize that this life is just a stepping stone, and your time here on Earth should be enjoyed because one day you will be moving on to your next adventure, you will let go of the stress and fear. When you accept responsibility for your own thoughts, words, and actions - and you forgive all others for theirs - you will truly evolve.

This lifetime is just that, a stepping stone that leads on to another and another...

So seek out the old souls and masters that walk among you, and watch them carefully. Follow your heart, intuition, and internal knowing. Let your actions in this lifetime lead you to the better stepping stones, the more enlightened adventures. Seek integrity, peace, and above all, seek love.

Rivers

Going with the flow, floating through your days without worry and doubt. How? Have you ever had the opportunity to spend time with someone that seemed totally relaxed, nothing seemed to upset them? They might have even moved at a slightly annoying pace. Did you feel annoyed, as if they didn't understand the urgency of life?

When you move quickly and try to accomplish as much as possible, are you happier? Or are you just distracted?

What happens when you are forced to slow down, to focus, or even worse, to just sit in silence? Like when you visit a doctor's office and are left in an exam room alone in silence. Does it put you on edge?

What is wrong with being calm? Many people wish and dream for peace. What is peace? Isn't it calm? Soothing, quiet, slow?

What do you truly crave?
What happened?
When did you become this driven personality?
What do you think contributes to this lifestyle?
Are you modeling your life after someone else's?
Will you achieve peace and joy if you are able to duplicate another's style and life?
Do you really want to be a copy or a duplicate?

You were created to be an original. Like no other, none, not a single copy of you should exist on Earth. Running around chasing after something that doesn't truly mean anything to you in the end...

Why? Ask yourself these questions and sit in silence and wait for the answers. I can assure you that before you took the leap to separate from me, you had a plan, we had a plan... let's get back to the plan. It is a really exciting adventure, and you can't fail if you just follow my cues. You know, your intuition, my guidance. But first you may need to slow down and strive for calm to avoid the many distractions that have led you away from all you were meant to be...

Find your flow and lose the struggle.

Just float and follow the river of life.

And when the water gets rough, hang on, that's part of the adventure. Just enough excitement to complement the calm.

Mountains

When your life feels like it is all uphill, and you are trudging one step after another feeling like you will never reach the top, wondering if you really want to keep going, you often stop. You look around and begin to compare your journey to the others that surround you on your path, and it seems they are passing you by. Years ago you thought you would easily beat everyone else to the top of the ladder, the hill, or the mountain. You had it all together, or so you thought. Steady finishes the race and even wins it sometimes. Your journey should not feel this way, with a lack of joy and excitement.

But there are times when your days will be filled with struggle and even suffering. How long you spend in this mindset depends entirely on how well you are able to realize that change is constant, and this moment was created by your past actions.

The good news is now obvious: what you do in this very moment will alter your path tomorrow. Maybe only slightly, but every action you take in a better direction will eventually lead you to a better place.

Perhaps you were walking on a spiral path up the side of the mountain, taking the long way that was less strenuous. Today, try a more difficult path, one that everyone else is not meandering about on, and put in a few extra steps straight up the side of that obstacle.

Then you will sleep well, satisfied that you put forth all of the effort you could today. And when you wake, you will continue not only to climb the mountain to see the top, but to grow stronger and more resilient, ready to embrace any challenges that come your way.

Those paths that are less traveled are filled with treasures yet to be discovered.

oxygen

Twisting and turning around you, life can bring forth quite a few challenges. Some expected, but others enough to knock you completely off balance, leaving you stunned.

What happens when you find yourself knocked off balance? Perhaps you become a bit stressed about something or someone that is actively challenging you, and you find yourself feeling out of sorts. The goal is to always remain balanced and calm and able to make decisions to lead you away from such circumstances.

For example, if you lose your job, it is easy to immediately fill yourself with doubt about your future. You may even begin to berate yourself or the person that let you go from your position. Your ego mind takes over, defending yourself instead of honestly analyzing the situation and looking for the opportunity that this new obstacle is presenting.

To you this isn't the easiest thing to do due to the high level of negative emotions that will be pushed forth from your egoistic mind.

But if you can take a moment to gather your thoughts - all of the negative ones - and put them aside for now, you will move through the emotions.

In the moment when you are most shocked, breathe.

Center yourself and breathe, realizing that your world is not actually caving in, you did not just fall off of a cliff. You are literally still alive and well.

You have only had a change in circumstance. There is an expression, "Rejection is God's protection." This is true and can be applied more often than you know.

Things happen in your day-to-day life, and when they do, the first thing you often do is go into a discordant breathing rhythm.

As silly as it may sound to you, your breathing truly regulates your heart and mind.

When you focus on slowly and calmly
inhaling and exhaling, you will not
only regain your balance but also your
composure and dignity.
It sounds simple.
But calm people live longer
and have happier lives.

They have mastered the breathing
techniques that enable them to expel
stress and anxiety leading to not only
easier days, but also better health and
well-being.

Oxygen.

It's that simple.

Leaves

Things come and go along your life journey. Like trees that go through the seasons with leaves coming and going, you will have souls that will cross your path that you will often need to sever ties with to avoid continued pain and suffering. And at other times, souls are removed from your life via distance or death.

Some souls drift slowly away hardly noticed, while others seem to be ripped out leaving grief and sorrow.

Knowing that this can happen often leads you to allow fear to control who you let into your life. After experiencing loss, you begin to base your current relationships on what has taken place in the past.

You may encourage others to "give everyone a chance," but do you follow that advice?

Trust your instinct, your intuition, your in-the-moment guidance, but evaluate based on what is presented in front of you, not what has been in your past.

Trees lose their leaves and new ones fill their places. Without questioning, the tree allows all of the leaves to grow without bias.

Do you allow all of the souls that cross your path an equal opportunity to enrich your life? Or do you shut them out in the name of protecting yourself?

Protect yourself through evaluation and prayer, but not to the extent that you sit alone untrusting of everyone.

There is a way to be careful without isolating yourself. Today look around and evaluate, are you too fearful based on your past? Or have you mastered the ability to evaluate a relationship, giving it the opportunity to slowly build and grow?

Water

What gives you strength and stamina? What rids your body of disease? What helps oxygenate your cells? What relaxes your system? What cleanses your body inside and out?

Water.

Like air, so important, yet often avoided and replaced with toxic substances including soda, alcohol, and other sugary drinks.

Pure, clean water is the foundation of your body. A simple drink. Just plain, it can be cold or room temperature to be enjoyed.

Around the world there are souls that go without clean water, something so basic and necessary for life. But if you are reading these words, I will imagine you have access to copious amounts of this amazing substance.

Some of you do try to stay hydrated, but most do not. I could lecture the many additional reasons why it is such a beneficial liquid, but your free will drives you, and my promise to not interfere teeters on these words. So instead, I just remind you of the benevolence of water.

Simple, yet refined. One of the few things you need to survive, and easily accessed to thrive.

But if I were you, well more than just a spark within you, I would delve into the habits encouraged in this book. Why not? You have nothing to lose except your health and well-being.

The simplicity of pure, clean water
exemplifies the organic structure
of balance and wellness that
abounds for you.

And yet, many substitute this
healing substance for toxic
liquids, attempting to quench
a non-existent thirst created by
marketing and greed.

Light

Brighter than the sun, the spark within you burns to energize your system, to bring life to your physical body. It is a spark like no other, something embedded within your soul, and within your DNA. Difficult to pinpoint, like electricity running web-like throughout your existence, this energy propels you forward in what you call time. This light surrounds you, appealing to the dark, as a whisp of cool air soothes you on a hot and humid day.

This divine light energy protects you, propels you, and enables you to be alive in this world.

It also links you to Me. You are a light soul, a being or substance of sorts that originated from Me. Your power is great once you begin the final journey of your return home. The closer you arrive, the more you understand and realize your thoughts, and your consciousness drives your reality.

Your spark of light lifts the veil for you to see the truth to find your way.

And the closer you travel in your thoughts and intentions to Me, the more you will shine through your physical body. Nothing will be able to stop you, your existence is eternal once you travel home. And this is possible without death - it is possible by understanding the relationship we have with one another.

The only way I know for you to get to know Me is to spend time with Me, I am here. I am always here, waiting for you to reach out with the intention of connecting.

Flowers

Draining yourself day after day, maneuvering your way through the daily obstacles that you come in contact with along your path, how exhausting. How frustrating this must be, wondering when your life will get better. Wondering who will arrive to save the day.

Looking at your current situation, are you the only one with this perspective of your challenges, does anyone else see things exactly as you do with the same passion or disheartenment? If you alone have the most enthralled perspective, then you, dear one, are the keeper of the solution.

You must come to your own rescue. And who better than you? You know what you want your life to be like, so start there and work backwards to create a plan.

If you want beautiful flowers to arrive just for you, it is much easier to grow them yourself than to rely on another soul to share your same vision. A simple example, but an important one to consider. When you plant your own garden and nurture it by putting your energy into the growth of the flowers, you will indeed benefit from your efforts.

Planting and nurturing one idea at a time will lead you to a better tomorrow. Use your will to live to rescue yourself.

Simply,
this is your journey.
This is your story.
Your thoughts create the
outcomes.
You are the hero.
Perhaps it is time you rescue
yourself.

Direction

Rotating, pivoting, or turning away from something unhealthy or risky is a natural survival skill. Your organic alert system built within you has the ability to save you from any threat.

It is less of a detector than a system to enhance your ability to know when to move away from an energy or type of activity. It does not always show you the physical form of the danger, it often only gives you a feeling or a small incongruent thought that does not align with your knowing of the situation.

In a given situation, it manifests as a feeling that something is off. Something does not sit well with you, but you can not pinpoint exactly what that something is to prove your decision to pivot and go in another direction.

Without physical proof, this leaves you with doubt. And often instead of trusting your unseen alert, you will continue in the direction of danger or malice intended to distract you at the least or do away with you at the worst.

What if you trusted yourself more than any other human on the planet?

What an obscure thought.

But take a moment to truly engage with the question. Is there one person, one soul, that you know in physical form that you can undoubtedly trust? Without question, without wondering if they have your best interest at heart? Unfortunately, and sadly, the answer is no. It is part of the separation, each soul out on their own journey, learning their own lessons, and each developing at their own pace.

To give you another perspective, do you know what you are truly capable of doing in any given situation? Have your actions ever surprised you? Perhaps you were braver than you thought capable, or maybe you caved in quicker than you had hoped? I think it is fair to recognize that you do not know how you will react in the most difficult situations, and therefore you are unable to proclaim that you know what you are capable of doing.

With this idea established, it becomes obvious that if you do not know what you are capable of, then you could not possible know what any other soul on their journey is capable of acting out.

Unless, of course, you are all acting under divine direction. Free will gives you the ability to choose who you take your direction from.

Choose wisely.

Sound

The distraction of sound leads you to be constantly manipulated without your knowing. From the music in stores to the sounds vibrating from your radios and movies, these sounds shape an important part of your being. The sound waves reverberate throughout your cells, often creating a discordant atmosphere that is so far on the spectrum from the glorious sounds that emanate from your natural vocal cords. These sounds wreak havoc on your system. All the while, you have been told that any music is good for you.

But like foods, organic is so much better for your system. Your bodies were not man-made, they connect best with natural matter. Whether this is natural clothing, organic foods, pure water, or harmonious frequencies.

Sounds that are calming and protective of your health are what your cells align and function best with, but today you are surrounded by the most chaotic sounds.

I can not interfere, but I can suggest doing your own experiment. Spend one day surrounding yourself with the normal sounds of your environment and note your overall emotions at the end of the day. Then try a full day focusing on "clean" sounds, calm music, even singing to yourself or humming all day. Note the difference.

Choosing what to surround yourself with includes the choice of sounds, and oh, what an effect they have. Seek the beautiful music that comes from the soul, that heals the soul, that brings the soul to life.

It is often the things in your life that have gone partially unnoticed that bring about the biggest change.

Like foods, organic sounds are
better for your system.

Your cells align and function
best with natural, harmonious
sounds.

Space

Where do you fit in? Do you know deep in your heart that I set a space for you during this time? I know there are days where you feel somewhat lost and confused, but it is how you continue forward that matters most to me. Time does not exist, only this moment is alive in you. And this is the place I hold space for your soul, this eternal moment called now. It truly lasts forever.

You have heard the advice from others perhaps, to stay present in the now. That is Me, that is you, we are now. The beginning and end all in one. Now.

I have saved this space for you. Just for you. To be in connection with Me, now.

I hope this is not confusing.

It makes perfect sense to Me, but I see humanity struggle with the concept that each soul is of vast importance to Me. And I wait patiently, always, eternally, for you to join me in the now to create together.

Earthquakes

What has the ability to shake your world? Not literally like an earthquake, but what types of things do you worry about disrupting your life? Things you might consider devastating?

> Loss of a loved one?
> Divorce or heartbreak?
> Illness?
> Losing your job? Your home?
> The list goes on and on...

How often do you think of these potential earthquake scenarios?

How much energy do you put into them?

When you worry, you attract earthquakes. They start with a warning, a tremor of sorts, and then if you expand your fear and continue to worry, the tremors increase until the big event is drawn into your life.

From my perspective, it seems so simple to avoid thinking about fearful outcomes. Especially when the world is filled with so many other wonderful, vibrant possibilities.

But I am not surrounded with constant manipulation and deceit and other souls telling me how horrible things are in your world.

I am surrounded by Angelics, benevolent beings that love, only love.

Who are you surrounded by? It makes a difference.

It is much easier to focus on rainbows and unicorns when you are not constantly pushing away thoughts of possible destruction.

Creating a sensible boundary for yourself would help alleviate the loss of energy felt from constantly trying to convince others to see things your way. When you act in regard for the highest good of all, you have the privilege of being right. But this by no means equates to being believed.

Sometimes you must stand alone when you are right. But are you really alone? There are other souls that will see your bravery and will eventually stand with you when they see it is safe.

You will bring balance to the world stage. Stand in your knowing that your heart guides you, and as long as you act with compassion and love for the highest good of all, you will be protected.

There comes a time when doing what others are afraid to do is the thing that frees you all.

This is now, when seeking and speaking the truth is the first step.

What follows will bring great benefit to humanity. Now that's something worth striving for...

Love

What exactly is love? It can't be captured, bottled, or boxed up. It exists all around you, yet often feels as though you can't quite reach it. Why is that?

Perhaps your definition is different than the way I would define love. I would define love as everything and nothing. The energy of compassion, patience, honesty, integrity, respect, hope, joy, anticipation, and the list goes on.

Acceptance is love.

I am love.

Forgiveness is love.

You are love.

Love is all that is good.

I am good.

You are good.

Love is the beginning and end.

Love is now.

This is now.

This is love.

It is so simple, yet misunderstood.

If you can accept good, and accept it now, then you can accept love.

Don't over-complicate it with trade-offs and wishes and demands. Love is simple, not grandiose.

Love simply is.

Accepting love as simply being is a start.

With love you create more love.

And with more love, the atmosphere changes for the better. It is the best "thing" to create with, it is unending, always in supply and the purest energy that exists.

Love, completely divine and completely All.

Thoughts

The most powerful tool you have to change your reality is your thoughts. Your concentrated, focused intentions (thoughts) hold the frequency to manipulate even matter. Start small with thoughts to change your emotional balance. Having a stressful moment? Overcome with worry? You may think of it as avoiding the trouble, but swiftly pivoting away from those dark emotions to emotions like hope and courage will bring you closer to a joyful resolution every time.

And this is only the beginning of what your thoughts do for you and to you. Approaching a situation with fear will leave you with anxiety and nervousness that can become debilitating. You have heard of a panic attack?

Turning those emotions loose into the atmosphere instead of allowing them to have a feeding frenzy on your nervous system and cells will allow you to breathe and realize you hold the answers to overcome anything that comes before you.

Let's talk about illness. Your innate body listens to your thoughts and follows the commands of the spoken word. Focus on illness and you will attract it, focus on health and you will enjoy life without disease.

Learn to control your own thoughts, steering them always in the direction of love, and you will reap the benefits.

As simple as it reads upon this page...create thoughts from a heartfelt place of love, and you will thrive.

My advice to you is direct and simple.

Create with love. Every thought, every word spoken, and every action taken – with love.

Your thoughts are your superpower.

Use your power for good.

Final Messages...

Remember you are love.

You are light.

You are the connection needed
to bring peace.

Once you see and accept
the perfection in others,
you will embrace your own true self.

When you accept responsibility
for your own thoughts, words,
and actions - and you forgive all
others for theirs - you will finally
be free.

Are you modeling your life after
someone else's? Do you really
want to be a copy or a duplicate?
Find your flow and lose the
struggle.

The good news is now obvious:
what you do in this very moment
will alter your path tomorrow.

In the moment when you are
most shocked - breathe. You will
not only regain your balance but
also your composure and dignity.

Leaves

Do you allow all of the souls
that cross your path an equal
opportunity to enrich your life?
Or,
do you shut them out in the name
of protecting yourself?

Water

**The simplicity of pure, clean
water exemplifies the organic
structure of balance and wellness
that abounds for you.**

This divine light energy
protects you, propels you, and
enables you to be alive in this
world.

Flowers
Simply,
this is your journey.
This is your story.
Your thoughts create the
outcomes.
You are the hero.
Perhaps it is time you rescue
yourself.

What if you trusted yourself
more than any other human on
the planet?
Listen to your heart, not your
ego.

**Your cells align and function
best with natural, harmonious
sounds.**

This space has been saved for
you. Just for you - to join me now
to create together.

When you act in regard for the
highest good of all, you have the
privilege of being right. But, this
by no means equates to being
believed.

The energy of earthquakes is
divisive. Seek unity instead.

Create with love.
Every thought,
every word spoken,
and every action taken - with love.
Do this and you will thrive.

Please help me share these
messages to inspire others to live
a more joyful life by sharing this
book with a friend.

For other books written with
messages from Source and for
daily/weekly messages, please visit
my website for social media links
or email me directly.

Thank you!

Love to you on your journey.

Carrington Allen
CarringtonAllen.com
carringtonsemail@gmail.com